Curious George®

The Perfect Carrot

Adaptation by Marcy Goldberg Sacks
Based on the TV series teleplay
written by Joe Fallon

Houghton Mifflin Harcourt Publishing Company
Boston   New York   2009

For information about permission to reproduce selections from this book, write to Permissions, Houghton Mifflin Harcourt Publishing Company, 215 Park Avenue South, New York, New York 10003.

Library of Congress Cataloging-in-Publication Data is on file.

ISBN: 978-0-547-24299-6

Design by Afsoon Razavi and Marcy Goldberg Sacks
www.hmhbooks.com
Manufactured in China
LEO 10 9 8 7 6 5 4 3 2 1

Today was a special day.
George was helping Bill feed his bunnies.
The bunnies loved carrots.

George ran out of carrots.
Where could he get more?
Bill pulled a carrot from the ground!
George was curious.
"You can grow carrots too," Bill said.
"You just need carrot seeds."

The man with the yellow hat gave
George a packet of seeds.
They read the directions.

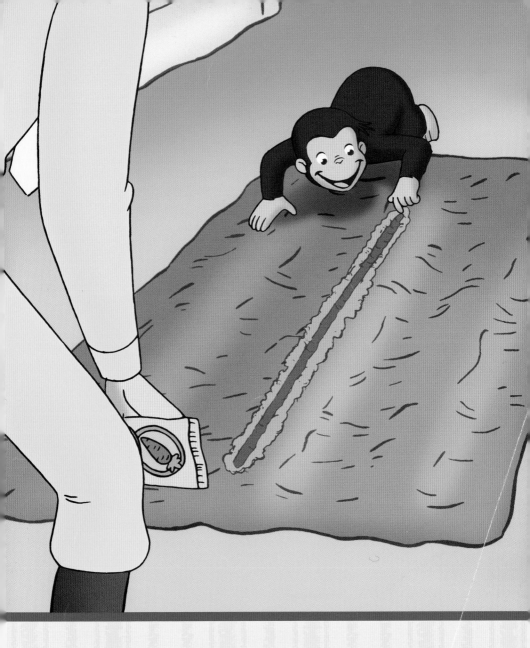

First, George dug a long hole in the ground.

Then he dropped
the seeds in one by one.
The man helped George cover the
seeds with dirt.

George watered them.
Dirt, water, and sunlight.
The seeds had everything they
needed to grow.

The next day there were no carrots.
George was confused.
"Carrots do not grow in one day,"
the man explained.
"Take good care of them every day.
They will grow in time."

George watered his carrots every day.
They started to grow.

George could not wait to see
his carrots.
He even dreamed about them.

After many weeks the carrots were ready.

George pulled them out of the ground.
Some of them looked funny.
But this one was perfect!

"Let's eat the carrot tonight!"
the man said.
But George wanted to save his carrot.
He put it in a case to keep it safe.

George went to show Bill his perfect
carrot. But Bill wasn't home.
A sign on the door said the bunnies
were missing!

George saw bunny footprints in
Bill's garden.
He followed them.

The footprints
led into a cave.
There were the bunnies!
They were lost and hungry.

George gave the bunnies his carrot.
While they ate, George went to
find Bill.

When they got
back to the cave,
the bunnies were still there.
But George's carrot was almost gone!

George did not mind.
His carrot was a hero—it had saved
the bunnies and the day!

Where Does Food Come From?

George grew fresh and delicious carrots right in his backyard. Did you know that a lot of the food we eat travels across the country in trucks, airplanes, and boats from very far away? A typical carrot has to travel more than 1,500 miles just to reach your dinner table!

Even if you can't grow your own vegetables like George, you can buy vegetables that are just as fresh and delicious from a local farm. Food you buy from a local farm is fresher, tastes better, and is healthier than food shipped long distances from other states or countries because the food doesn't spend days in trucks and stores losing nutrients.

Next time you go to the grocery store, see whether there is a sign for locally grown vegetables next to the other vegetables. Or ask an adult to find out if there is a farm near where you live. Call the farm to see when they're open and what they're selling. Many farms will schedule tours, and some even let you pick your own vegetables. Maybe you'll find a carrot as perfect as the one that George grew!

USDA Economic Research Service. "Farm Numbers/Largest Growing Fastest." *Agricultural Outlook*, October 2002.

Cooking with Carrots!

Did you know that you can cook delicious desserts with carrots? Ask an adult to help you with this yummy recipe for carrot muffins.

Here are the ingredients you will need:

1 ½ cups flour

2 teaspoons of cinnamon

1 ½ teaspoons of baking powder

½ teaspoon of baking soda

½ teaspoon of salt

3 medium eggs

¾ cup of granulated sugar

1 ½ cups of shredded carrots

½ cup of raisins or walnuts

½ cup of milk

½ cup of melted butter

Follow these steps:

1. Preheat your oven to 400° F.
2. Combine the flour, cinnamon, baking powder, baking soda, and salt.
3. In a separate bowl, beat together the eggs and the granulated sugar.
4. Add the shredded carrots, raisins or walnuts, milk, and butter; mix well.
5. Add the flour mixture and stir until the wet and dry ingredients are mixed completely.
6. Spoon the batter into twelve greased muffin cups.
7. Bake for 20 minutes.

Optional Frosting

Ingredients:

¼ cup of cream cheese, softened

1 tablespoon of melted butter

1 cup of powdered sugar

2 tablespoons of milk

½ teaspoon of vanilla

1. Mix together cream cheese and butter.
2. Stir in the powdered sugar, milk, and vanilla, and then drizzle over the top of the cooked muffins.